Still Time to Pray

PRAYERS
& PRAISE
FOR LATE
IN LIFE

Still Time to Pray

Catharine Brandt

AUGSBURG Publishing House • Minneapolis

STILL TIME TO PRAY

Contents

Preface

Many older Christians still use their skills and talents. Others with less prominent gifts or with ebbing physical strength may feel disqualified.

But God has given his followers a gift to be used for his glory to the close of life—*prayer*.

Even with failing eyesight or impaired hearing, in a hospital bed or wheelchair, day or night, for as long as God grants us clear minds, we can pray.

Prayer is a gift great characters of the Bible seized and wrestled with; then they praised God for results. Like Moses, we can pray for others. Hannah's prayer was for her personal need. Elijah prayed for victory over enemies of God. David praised God after repentance. The writer of Hebrews urges us to draw near to God with confidence that we may find mercy and grace to help in time of need (Heb. 4:16 RSV). God hears us when we pray in Jesus' name.

The prayers in this book may be used as suggestions for your prayers. They may remind you of someone you have neglected to pray for, or you may think of others not named here.

You might like to write in the margins the names of those you pray for. If, when God answers your prayers, you mark "praise" beside the request, this book can be a continuing record of your prayers and praise.

For Self

Let us test and examine our ways, and return to the Lord!

Lamentations 3:40 RSV

Stumbler

Lord, today I'm first in line.
In a moment I'll pray for others;
now it's time to talk about me.
I am unsure of what lies ahead.
You know the temptations
that will entangle my feet,
the troubles that will weigh me down.
If it's too much for you
to change the circumstances,
please change me.
You know I'm a stumbler
in rocky places.
Safeguard me with courage.
If I'm at the bottom of the heap,
or bruised and on top,
please lend a hand.
Set me upright.
Thank you for past rescues
and your promise for today.

**Fear not, for I am with you, be not dismayed,
for I am your God; I will strengthen you,
I will help you, I will uphold you with my
victorious right hand (Isa. 41:10 RSV).**

New Career

I think of that woman
who just finished seminary.
She's over 65 and
wants to serve a country church.
They can't afford to pay much,
but she doesn't care about money.
She wants to preach your Word
and help people.
Lord, I'm retired,
but I'm not past wanting to serve you.
Your Book teaches
one is never too old, too weak,
too discouraged to pray.
Heavenly Father, I'm willing.
I have the time for a prayer career.
Give me the determination
to stick with it.
Let your Spirit whisper to me
the ones you want me to pray for.

Seek the Lord and his strength, seek his face continually (1 Chron. 16:11 KJV).

Expectancy

Lord, I want to pray
with my heart, my mind.
Don't let me take a vacation
as I kneel in your presence.
Don't let me do all the talking;
I need to listen.
Help me gather my scattered thoughts
into a time of waiting
and receiving.

When I take time to pray and listen,
you shower me with benefits:
strength to obey your commands,
comfort for sorrow,
direction at crossroads,
the presence of your Holy Spirit,
joy bells within.

But they who wait for the Lord
shall renew their strength,
they shall mount up with wings like eagles,
they shall run and not be weary,
they shall walk and not faint (Isa. 40:31
RSV).

Winter Discipline

Give me a northern apple
in winter's icy siege—
cardinal red, hiding
sweet-sharp nourishment.

Outside my window
bare-branched apple trees
shiver in freezing blasts,
storing strength
for spring blossoms,
harvest fruit.

Lord, have you planted me
in a winter place
that I might bear fruit?

I am the vine, you are the branches. He who abides in me, and I in him, he it is that bears much fruit, for apart from me you can do nothing (John 15:5 RSV).

More Like the Master

Sometimes I think
I'm on the shelf, out of it,
no longer useful.
Then you remind me
I still have the wit
to be kind,
to forgive,
to make peace with others,
to be friendly.
Help me not to be prickly
nor complaining
with the people around me.
Instead, enable me to give love.

And walk in love, as Christ loved us and gave himself up for us, a fragrant offering and sacrifice to God (Eph. 5:2 RSV).

I Never Did That Before

Head down, I stagger along
ruts carved in wagon days,
    old habits.
Fresh winds of change
blow across my footpath.
New versions of your Word,
innovative mergers.
Young Christians detached
from worldly goods,
soaring to new heights
of selflessness.

Savior, you spoke of radical ideas.
Scoop me out of my rut.
I long to be airborne,
to travel sky-flights of liberty,
slice through fog and clouds
to blue-sky clarity.
Help me learn from
young followers of yours.

**Live as free men, but do not use your freedom
as a cover-up for evil; live as servants of God
(1 Peter 2:16 NIV).**

Reflection

My shoulder aches.
Bills add up to more
than my bank balance.
They raised the rent.
Inflation lurks.
My neighbor turned her back.
A stranger laughed at me.

But neighbors are watching,
strangers too,
to see how I will act
in pain and conflict.
Father, give me your strength.
Let my words and actions
reflect your unfailing love.

My deep desire and hope is that I shall never fail in my duty, but that at all times, and especially right now, I shall be full of courage, so that with my whole being I shall bring honor to Christ, whether I live or die (Phil. 1:20 TEV).

Hypocrite Needing Renewal

Some rob banks, hijack planes,
peddle drugs or pornography,
cheat widows, commit murder.
I thank you, God, that's not me.

I turn a green eye on prosperous friends.
I whisper gossip behind my hand.
I lie—bold and outright,
white and undercover.
I nurse grudges,
close ears to cries of poor and hungry.

O God, have mercy.
Don't allow my sins
to cut me off from you.
Thank you for your grace
that forgives and restores me.

**Search me, O God, and know my heart: try
me and know my thoughts: and see if there
be any wicked way in me, and lead me in the
way everlasting (Ps. 139:23-24 KJV).**

Joyful Noise

Lord, I feel like singing,
not exactly grand opera,
just a heart melody.
Thank you for hymn writers
who set Christian truths to music.
Thank you for people who
sing your praise
tunefully or off-key.
Thank you for David,
sweet singer of Israel,
who rejoiced in music.
Thank you for parents
who implant a song
in little children's hearts
and teach them to sing.
Music makes the day brighter.
Thank you we never grow
too old to sing your praises.

**Make a joyful noise to the Lord, all the lands!
Serve the Lord with gladness!
Come into his presence with singing! (Ps.
100:1-2 RSV).**

Hello, God

You are always on the spot.
No need to wait
or take a number.
The line to your ear
is never busy.
Your eyes are never asleep
to my need.
I don't have to be in church,
or come for supplies
only when the store is open.
You are nearby day and night.
And everything is free.
Lord, keep me from turning away
from the riches of your love.

The eyes of the Lord are upon the righteous, and his ears are open unto their cry (Ps. 34:15 KJV).

For Parents and Children

Sons are a heritage from the Lord,
children a reward from him.

Psalm 127:3 NIV

Blessings on a New Life

She placed her small son in my arms,
incredibly heavy for three months old.
I saw the blue sweater rise and fall
with each tiny heartbeat.
Round eyes watched me.
Conversation grew one-sided
until he smiled
and answered me
in an unknown tongue.

Giver of all life,
what lies ahead
for this little new one?
Grant that his parents
will instruct him
in your commands and love.
Make him teachable
and keep him for your purposes.

. . . from childhood you have been acquainted
with the sacred writings which are able to
instruct you for salvation through faith in
Christ Jesus (2 Tim. 3:15 RSV).

Dropout

Father in heaven,
my young friend
wants to drop out of school.
You know what keeps him from study.
Parents nagging?
  Loneliness?
    Not liking himself?
      Laziness?
You have given him a good mind.
Help counselors motivate him
to use that gift.
Help his parents remember the way it was
when they were young.
May they give encouragement,
not a sermon.
Confront him with his need
to trust you.

Let the word of Christ dwell in you richly in all wisdom; teaching and admonishing one another (Col. 3:16 KJV).

Step by Step

Lord, I never imagined
this giant trial for my dear one,
greater than any in the past.
Still, I remember you guided me
step by step through stormy paths
strewn with stumbling blocks.
Your grace was sufficient.
Not for next month,
   or next week,
      or tomorrow,
but grace for each obstacle.
Don't let my loved one
be a tumbleweed
whisked far from you by squally winds.
Give your strength.
May faith increase
through this calamity.

Thus far has the Lord helped us (1 Sam. 7:12 NIV).

Fresh Start

She is young to be a mother.
Long hair and jeans.
Life drained out of her eyes.
Alone.
Before her loom big decisions.
But she has made the crucial one—
she wants to start over.
She wants you to be in charge.
Loving Father, draw her to you.
When she wavers, gently lead her.
Set her feet in the right path.
Forbid that anyone should hinder
your work of grace.
Often you have built beauty out of ashes.
May she do her part.
Please give her family and friends
who will embrace her with love
and encouragement.

And be kind to one another, tenderhearted, forgiving one another, as God in Christ forgave you (Eph. 4:32 RSV).

Prayer for Fathers

Teal-feather hooded,
a mallard strutted near my path
(though I was near his turf
had I but known).
The duck stood still,
forbidding my advance.
No need to take my measure.
My shoes outlined against green grass
spelled danger.
Boldly he scolded me
for venturing too close
to hidden mother duck and ducklings.

How often I have noted human fathers,
bold by necessity,
feeding and protecting
their young families,
warding off the enemy.
Keep them vigilant, Lord,
alert to sudden hazards.
Give them boldness to rout enemies.
In the name of Jesus, who taught us
the true meaning of father.

**As a father has compassion on his children,
so the Lord has compassion on those who
fear him (Ps. 103:13 NIV).**

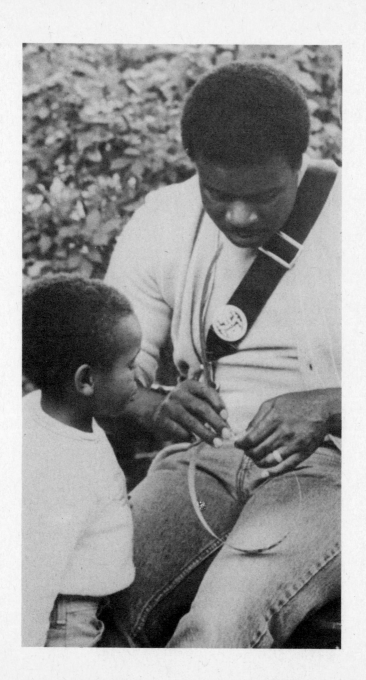

Battered Families

Our times are "out of joint"
when large and powerful adults
can get away with physically harming
little children and women.
Are the strong ones battered children too?
Hurting in ways they can't express
except by violence?

Jesus invited crowds to come to him.
He taught the good news
that people can be reconciled to God.
His disciples fanned out
with the message.

Loving God, may your Spirit
repeat the pattern today.
Draw men and women to you.
Send them into crowded cities
with the good news.
Heal those who hurt, I pray.

Be sober, be watchful. Your adversary the
devil prowls around like a roaring lion,
seeking someone to devour (1 Peter 5:8
RSV).

Plans

Something is happening
to my dear one,
something I can't control.
I want to, Lord.
I'm eager to advise, admonish,
offer plans—to act.
Help me sit on my hands,
keep my mouth shut,
so I don't try to help you out.
My resources add down to zero.
You calmed raging seas,
performed miracles,
quieted disciples' fears.
Give me faith
to allow you
to work your plans
in my dear one's life.

Many are the plans in a man's heart, but it is the Lord's purpose that prevails (Prov. 19:21 NIV).

Diploma

Brass band crashing,
pomp and circumstance,
graduates marching,
honors, awards, speeches.
After the solemnity,
hilarity, freedom!
Thank you, God,
for the milestone of graduation.
Thanks for all who remembered to pray,
teachers who opened doors of knowledge,
parents who stood by
with reproof and advice
(and sympathy and love
and chocolate chip cookies).
Thanks for young people
who hung in there to the end.
As they plunge into new ventures,
may they know the freedom
of God's mercy and forgiveness
through Christ the Savior.

**So if the Son makes you free, you will be
free indeed (John 8:36 RSV).**

For Friends
and Neighbors

A friend loves at all times.

Proverbs 17:17 RSV

Surprise

Lord, I like the surprises
you tuck into my days.
Sometimes I find friends
in unexpected places—
like my special friend
who is in a nursing home.
A stroke damaged her vocal chords.
Talking is difficult,
but her face shines
with love and humor.
We like each other.
Before her move she asked you
to give her one good friend.
"And here you are," she says.

Lord, I'm humbled
that she counts me
that one good friend.
By your Spirit show me ways
to be sensitive to her needs.
Thank you for the gift of friendship.

Two are better than one; because they have a good reward for their labour (Eccl. 4:9 KJV).

Wedding Guest's Prayer

God bless the young people
starting marriage today.
Grant that they will put Jesus first
in their home.
Where one has a weakness,
let the other be strong.
Where there is illness or trouble,
let them turn to you in prayer.
When anger boils over,
lead them to your Book.
Teach them commitment
to each other
and to you.
May they smile and laugh
and weep together
while they store tender memories
for future joy.

**Therefore shall a man leave his father and
his mother, and shall cleave unto his wife:
and they shall be one flesh (Gen. 2:24 KJV).**

Divorce

Your Book tells us
you meant a husband and wife
to stay together till death.
No divorce.
I pray for my neighbors
who have split apart.
I didn't know how much sorrow
they had encountered.
Nor how miserable their home life,
how limited her physical strength,
how meager his weekly pay.
Forgive me, Lord, for not helping
when the need was great.
Now she has returned to the church
for comfort and direction.
Give her strength
to bear her crushing load.
Help us not to censor her.
Erase our prejudice, Lord.
Show us how to open our arms
and take her in.
Lord, I pray, if possible,
you will turn the one who left around.

**Trust in the Lord with all your heart, and do
not rely on your own insight (Prov. 3:5 RSV).**

Perfect Gift

The young man across the street
has been laid off.
He can't afford that, Lord.
He has three children in school.
Please help him accept
these forced stay-at-home days
with cheerfulness
and faith in your grace.
Give him added love
for wife and children,
more love for you.
Direct friends to support him
with kindness
while he looks for work.
If he learns your grace
will see him through
that will be a greater gift
than a new job today.

My grace is sufficient for you (2 Cor. 12:9 RSV).

Friend

I hadn't known
it was a day of meeting.
I climbed the winding hill
of everyday-ness
unaware of approaching
an intersection.
In God's providence
our paths crossed.
That day he gave me
a friend.
My life is richer
for knowing
one who loves me
and leads me closer
to God's love.

I thank my God in all my remembrance of you (Phil. 1:3 RSV).

Across the Miles

This morning brought thoughts
of my friend half a continent away.
I wonder why, Lord?
We are out of touch,
no phone call,
no letter in the mail
to remind me of our friendship.
Just a mind picture,
bright and persistent.
Lord, have you signaled me to pray?
Is my friend afraid?
Lonely, sorrowful, ill?
Attacked by the enemy?
Turn the golden light of your love
full on my friend.
May your presence be felt.
Give joy and strength for the day.

. . . being strengthened with all power according to his glorious might so that you may have great endurance and patience (Col. 1:11 NIV).

Going in Circles

O God, often in the past
when attacked by the enemy
I struggled to work things out
like a rower with one oar out of the water.
I grumbled, worried,
forgot your promise
to lead me out of deep, choppy waters.
Then you showed me
your power in my weakness.

Now let your Spirit guide me
in what to say to a busy mother,
capable, energetic,
dizzy with action,
not wanting to sit with folded hands
and wait for your help.

Wait for the Lord; be strong, and let your heart take courage; yea, wait for the Lord! (Ps. 27:14 RSV).

Patterns

At times I want to remodel others.
When tempers flare,
unkind words erupt,
lawbreakers defy God,
I want to shake, scold.
Why can't they be more loving,
joyous, peaceful?
More like the Savior?
Where's their faith, their long-suffering?

Why do I think I'm in the repair business?
That my job is to improve others?
Your Word teaches the uniqueness
of your creatures.
No two zebras have the same stripes.
Snowflakes, petals, shells—each is unique.
Babies, too. And neighbors.
You are the Great Designer
and the Perfect Pattern.
Put me in my place, Lord.
Help me be a little pattern
of your love.

Yet, O Lord, you are our Father. We are the clay, you are the potter; we are all the work of your hand (Isa. 64:8 NIV).

For Strangers

As you did it to one of the least of these my brethren, you did it to me.

Matthew 25:40 RSV

Acceptance

He didn't look like other boys.
He didn't talk like them.
With imperfect gait
he stumbled, lurched.

Did his mother cradle him with adoration?
Did she envision genius for her son—
    at first?
Did it take long days and years
to learn acceptance,
to understand God gives
with purpose and love?

Forgive my careless rejection
of one of your children.
Give me joy and compassion
to reach out to mother and boy.
O Lord, hasten the day
when you will heal all flaws.

**It was not that this man sinned, or his
parents, but that the works of God might
be made manifest in him (John 9:3 RSV).**

Window on the World

It's not a picture window,
only a narrow one.
People scurry past
needing God's grace.
Let me choose one
to center my prayer upon.
That tall stranger-boy,
hair over eyes, reedy neck,
loping across the street.
O God, give him purpose
in his life.
If he's at a crossroads,
show him the way to go.
May he submit to your authority.
I wonder what his name is?
No matter. You know.
Surround him with your love, I pray.

**How can a young man keep his way pure?
By guarding it according to thy word
(Ps. 119:9 RSV).**

Living with Conflict

When it comes to arguing and violence
I'm a conscientious objector.
Dear Father,
you know that wasn't always so.
I had to learn that we live with conflict.
Uncontrolled outbursts
never win a battle.
You taught me to allow others
to think and act in ways contrary to mine.
I pray for dissenters
on city streets and campuses.
Riots never prove who is right,
only "who is left after the battle."
Lord, we are a strange mix
of race, culture, language,
of believers in your Son Jesus
and children of disobedience.
Teach us how to live together,
in the Savior's name.

**If possible, so far as it depends upon you,
live peaceably with all (Rom. 12:18 RSV).**

Turnabout

At times I don't want
to listen to newscasts.
   Arson
      head-on collisions
         murders
            rapes
               robberies.
Yet victims and villains
both need prayer.
May those who have been hurt
feel your tenderness.
Is it too late for the ones
who caused pain and suffering
to turn from darkness to light?
O Lord, confront them
with judgment
and their need to repent.

**Giving thanks to the Father . . . . For he
has rescued us from the dominion of
darkness and brought us into the kingdom
of the Son he loves, in whom we have
redemption, the forgiveness of sins
(Col. 1:12-14 NIV).**

New Church Member

He joined your church, Lord,
a new Christian
struggling to climb out
of the swampy bog of drugs.
He has trust and hope in his eyes,
a song in his heart,
and praise on his lips.
Don't let him falter
with discouragement
when he learns
the Christian life is costly.
Your Son spoke of
   a cross
     denial
       service
         a crown—and joy!
May we help him
and teach him joy
in the Christian life.

**For the kingdom of God is not a matter of
eating and drinking, but of righteousness,
peace and joy in the Holy Spirit
(Rom. 14:17 NIV).**

Day's End

Lord, I've laid aside
shoes and clothing
ready for sleep.
But not quite.
I failed the test today.
Face-to-face with trial,
I refused to "count it all joy."
The trial loomed too big to tackle.
My faith wobbled.
I ran away.

And that's not all, Lord.
I'm cloaked with grudges.
Others needing my time and money,
strangers' mistakes,
unkept promises.
I lay resentment aside.
In Jesus' name
I plead for forgiveness.
Now come, sleep.

**For if you forgive men their trespasses,
your heavenly Father also will forgive you
(Matt. 6:14 RSV).**

Behind Bars

Lord, they're in prison
because they broke the law,
punishment intended
to compensate for lawlessness.
Locked in by violence,
hardened hearts,
high walls,
how can they be salvaged?
Thank you for men and women
working for better conditions
in prisons.
Thank you for counselors
who teach and preach
the good news of salvation
to prisoners.
Lord Jesus, you can calm
evil forces inside prison walls
as you calmed the sea long ago.
You can soften hearts so the gospel
sets them free,
even behind bars.

**Now the Lord is the Spirit, and where the
Spirit of the Lord is, there is freedom
(2 Cor. 3:17 RSV).**

Low-Key Witness

Heavenly Father, protect your church
in countries of political turmoil,
where secret followers of Jesus,
underground worshipers,
are not allowed to give Christian witness
in fear of their lives.

The shocker is
I sit at home,
read,
listen to rumblings,
remain silent.
Compel me to rise
from my comfortable chair,
to kneel and pray.
May your Spirit move about,
cause governments
to change policies,
provide for citizens' needs.
Grant that your children
will live the Christian life
so others will take note.

**For he who is in you is greater than he
who is in the world (1 John 4:4 RSV).**

For Teachers,
Preachers,
—and Missionaries—

The fear of the Lord, that is wisdom; and
to depart from evil is understanding.

Job 28:28 KJV

Apple for Teacher

Some teachers stand out,
like overhead freeway signs
pointing the right way.
Loving pupils and loving God,
they taught honesty,
opened peepholes
and skylights
into God's world.
Sparks jumped
from teacher to learner.
Heedless then,
I wish I might say thanks now.
But some have moved.
For others it is too late.
Did they ever surmise
unspoken appreciation, I wonder?

Master Teacher, bless today's teachers.
Give them extra strength,
patience, love, understanding.
Beautify the school year
with students who want to learn,
and who take time to say thanks.

**So teach us to number our days that we
may get a heart of wisdom (Ps. 90:12 RSV).**

Shepherd and Sheep

Lord, you have sent us a pastor
with a shepherd's heart,
not too busy with meetings and books
to care about his flock.
Thank you for one
who preaches your Word with simplicity
so little children understand,
who teaches older ones
to obey your commands.
He too needs prayer.
His shoulders are stooped with a heavy load
caused by scrawny, wandering sheep.
In times of weariness,
refresh him.
Protect him from Satan's attacks.
Gladden him with the knowledge
that he has turned ears and eyes
to that great shepherd of the sheep—
   the Lord Jesus.

**I am the good shepherd; I know my own
and my own know me (John 10:14 RSV).**

Send Workers

Lord, I've just listened to the news.
Millions hungry,
homeless,
violent,
hating each other,
not knowing the Savior's love.
You have told us to look
at fields ripe with crops.
I am too old, too weak to work.
Lord of the harvest,
speak to able young men and women.
Arouse them to look
at your fields,
to work in faraway lands
or at home
while there is time.

**The harvest is plentiful but the workers
are few. Ask the Lord of the harvest,
therefore, to send out workers into his
harvest field (Matt. 9:37-38 NIV).**

In a Strange Land

Thank you, God, for missionaries,
men and women willing to leave home
and strike out for a strange land.
I pray for
newly appointed missionaries.
When homesickness engulfs them,
be the guest in their homes.
When regret pricks them,
brighten the day with your joy.
When language study wearies them,
let them trust in your omniscience.
If they should desire to change
customs that seem strange,
show them, instead,
they are only the pipeline
for life-changing good news.

**Go into all the world and preach the gospel
to the whole creation (Mark 16:15 RSV).**

Sunday Morning

He's a young minister, Lord,
unsure in the pulpit,
with little experience
   preaching
      teaching
         counseling.
And I have walked the way
for years.
But I have not come to your house
to criticize his fumbling words.
I've come to worship you.
I'm so aware of my need to be fed.
Arouse me with expectation.
Awaken me with your presence.
Give him some profound word
that I may take home
to meditate on this week.
Then school him daily, I pray.

**Enter into his gates with thanksgiving, and
into his courts with praise; be thankful unto
him, and bless his name (Ps. 100:4 KJV).**

I'll Pray for You

How dreamy, Lord, for missionaries
to go to foreign lands.
When I promised to pray,
I meant it.
But I've been busy—
until the letter came.
  Household goods have not arrived.
  Culture shock distresses.
  Ants overrun the kitchen.
Thank you for missionaries
who report honestly
what it's like to work for you
in another country.
Forgive my neglect.
Forgetting to pray
is like leaving the scene
of an accident.
Please cut through red tape.
Give them courage to withstand
big and little persecutions.

God forbid that I should sin against the Lord in ceasing to pray for you (1 Sam. 12:23 KJV).

Blazing Trails

O God, our Savior,
you demand action of your followers.
  Go into all the world.
      Preach the gospel.
          Feed the hungry.
But I am prisoned
in a small place,
my days for action over.
Ah! Lord, your Book
holds other demands.
    Come unto me.
        Fight the good fight of faith.
          Pray without ceasing.
I bow to learn your orders.
Please use me to encourage
ones with little faith,
to pray for those active
in your service.
Keep my laggard thoughts
centered on you.
Teach me to pray inwardly
moment by moment.

I will go in the strength of the Lord God (Ps. 71:16 KJV).

For Authorities
—and Helpers—

Let every person be subject to the governing authorities. For there is no authority except from God, and those that exist have been instituted by God.

Romans 13:1 RSV

A Lonely Man

Almighty God, your Word tells us
to pray for those in high places.
I pray for one with great authority—
our president,
your man of destiny.
Surround him with wise helpers.
When grave problems confront him,
grant that he will
ask wisdom of God.
When he faces momentous decisions,
may he not be a people-pleaser
but vote for what is right
even though he stands alone.
When others heap praise on him,
keep him humble.
When he walks in danger,
protect him.

**Wealth and honor come from you;
    you are the ruler of all things.
In your hands are strength and power
    to exalt and give strength to all
(1 Chron. 29:12 NIV).**

High Positions

Lord, you invite us
to a peaceable life.
But uproar and argument
assault our ears.
Lawbreakers and violence
threaten us.
Ruler of the universe,
empower our president
with wisdom, courage, integrity.
Impel Congress to legislate
reasonable laws.
Strengthen governors.
Give us honest businessmen
willing to boycott greed and selfish goals.
Make me prompt to obey
lawful authority.

**I urge that supplications . . . be made
for . . . kings and all who are in high
positions, that we may lead a quiet and
peaceable life, godly and respectful in
every way (1 Tim. 2:1-2 RSV).**

I Depend on People

Thank you, Lord, for people
who served me today:
  bag boy
  busboy
  fire fighter
  mail carrier
  police officer
  waitress.
Their service requires
quick strong muscles,
endurance and accuracy,
often bravery, taking risks,
and keeping their wits about them.
They need your love and care
to lift their spirits.
May they know the satisfaction
of jobs well done.

Whatever you do, in word or deed, do everything in the name of the Lord Jesus, giving thanks to God the Father through him (Col. 3:17 RSV).

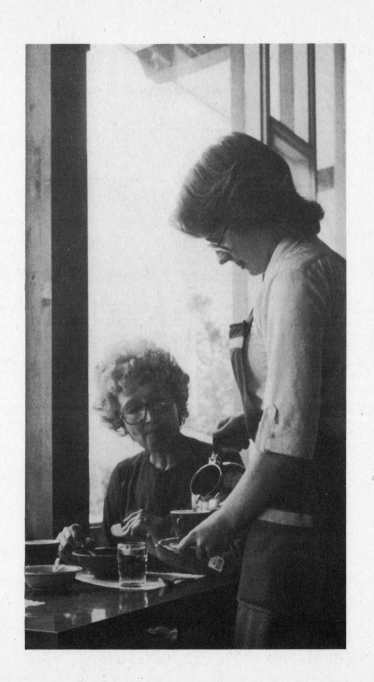

Officers of the Law

Thank you for police
directing traffic,
keeping peace on city streets,
protecting citizens
through dark of night.
Fearlessly they confront
lawbreakers and accidents.
Around corners, behind doors,
they often meet tragedy,
disaster.
Lord, keep their minds keen and alert.
Strengthen them in their duty.
Remind them they represent justice,
not brute power.
And Lord, as followers of Jesus,
keep us from disobeying the law.

Would you have no fear of him who is in authority? Then do what is good (Rom. 13:3 RSV).

Fasten Seat Belts

I praise you, God!
What a wonder it is
to fly across your world,
to enjoy blue sky
above fluffs of buoyant clouds.
I don't understand aeronautics
or mechanics
of sky-flight.
Nor what all the lights
and buttons are for.
I leave all that to the pilots,
trusting their skills
to hold our plane on course.

And yet, Lord,
please give the pilots a sure touch
as they operate the controls.
Give them awareness of
responsibility for human life.
Give them trust in your omnipotence.

**Some trust in chariots, and some in horses:
but we will remember the name of the Lord
our God (Ps. 20:7 KJV).**

Accountability

Thank you for your master plan.
Heredity, time, place,
and the gospel converged.
  America is my birthplace.
  I am alive this day of marvels.
  I am one of your daughters.
Despite America's faults and failures,
opportunity and liberty still hold true—
  for some.
O Lord, hasten the day
when you will return
to rule the earth with justice—
  for all.
In the meantime help us
stand shoulder to shoulder,
eager to help those in need,
giving liberally of what we have,
quick to follow your commands,
Author of Liberty.

**From everyone who has been given much,
much will be demanded (Luke 12:48 NIV).**

For the
Troubled, Sick,
and Bereaved

And God shall wipe away all tears from their eyes; and there shall be no more death, neither sorrow, nor crying, neither shall there be any more pain . . . .

Revelation 21:4 KJV

Miracle of Sleep

Often I take sleep
for granted,
as if day's end entitled me
to oblivion that renews.
Father, this night I thank you
for the miracle of sleep.
Be near your children
who will not sleep tonight.
Tossing with pain,
pacing with anxiety,
waiting for a loved one's return,
night turned to day
by job's demand.
Thank you, Lord, for peace
in the darkest night.
And should I lie awake,
let me recall
your goodness and mercy this day.

**I will lie down and sleep in peace, for you
alone, O Lord, make me dwell in safety
(Ps. 4:8 NIV).**

Count Blessings

Father, sometimes I forget
to thank you
for eyes that see,
ears that hear,
two good legs,
until you remind me
by a deaf woman,
a blind man,
one who uses a walker.
I did not know she stands
on artificial legs.
Lord, forgive my ingratitude.
Use my eyes, my ears, my legs
to help people who lack
gifts I take for granted.

I was eyes to the blind, and feet was I to the lame (Job 29:15 KJV).

Freely Give

Lord, my plate is full,
brimming with good food
from your bounty.
My heart is spilling over with thanks.
Yet I think of people
in other countries—
children with swollen bellies,
wide eyes of fear—
starving, dying.
Jesus saw the hungry
and gave them food.
Even though my resources are limited,
help me give what I can
to the hungry of your world
in the name of Jesus
who called himself the
Bread of Life.

**Freely you have received, freely give
(Matt. 10:8 NIV).**

The Plague

O God, it's such a dread disease,
striking terror in those
who hear the verdict,
despair in all
who suffer cancer's pain.
I pray for faithful scientists
testing, researching cause and cure.
Enlighten them.
Quicken powers of discovery.
I pray for baffled doctors and nurses,
for angry, questioning families.
Give them tenderness
for cancer patients.
Your Word tells us you have loved us
with an everlasting love.
You have the resources.
Nothing is hidden from you.
Alert us all, O God,
to our part in the fight
against cancer.

Ah, Sovereign Lord, you have made the heavens and the earth by your great power and outstretched arm. Nothing is too hard for you (Jer. 32:17 NIV).

Touch of Love

Lord, when you walked
this planet long ago,
you loved the untouchable,
the unclean,
even lepers.
You could have healed
the leper by command.
But you touched him.

You touched me
when I was needy
and unloveable.
Some of your children repel me.
Outcasts, downcasts,
tumbled down, sin-scarred,
needing your healing touch.
Teach me to touch them
with love.

For the Son of Man came to seek and to save the lost (Luke 19:10 RSV).

Appointment with God

Doctors say my friend
is terminally ill.
I feel helpless when
death stalks.
What does it mean to know
now is the time?
How can I comfort her?
Ease her pain and fears?
Your Word pictures a place
prepared for her in heaven.
No more pain or sorrow.
I'm going to miss her
when she is gone.
But as long as she lives
I want to love her
and do everything I can for her.

**When your days are fulfilled. . . .
(2 Sam. 7:12 RSV).**

Outsider

Loving Savior,
he is a lonely old man,
frail and frightened.
His children moved him
when his lifetime partner died.
They wanted him with people.
But people are groups,
    clans, cliques, families,
opening a tiny bit,
closing smoothly,
not letting outsiders in.

May your Spirit show me
how to help this lonely one.
You have taught me
to accept loneliness,
that it can be the door
to a bright tomorrow,
a closer walk with you
and your followers.
May this man feel loved by your church
and turn to you for contentment and joy.

**So in Christ we who are many form one
body, and each member belongs to all the
others (Rom. 12:5 NIV).**

Peace

Lord Jesus, you comforted me
through my dark valley.
In the pain of death
you taught me peace
in trusting you.

Please help me
comfort my neighbor
whose love
lies still within a box.
He's broken, Lord,
thinking only of his loss
and what might have been.
Teach him what is yet to be.
I too was slow to learn.
Help me reach out
with what I know
of acceptance and trust.
Give him what only you can give—
peace.

**God . . . comforts us in all our affliction,
so that we may be able to comfort those
who are in any affliction (2 Cor. 1:4 RSV).**

Your House, Lord

This place is called
a house of praise,
but now it is
a house of sorrow.
We never thought to see this one
once so alive, kind, joyful,
now toppled as a tree
uprooted by tornado.
The shock is like
a blow against the stomach.
O God, in this house of sorrow
may the brokenhearted
hear your promises
of love and comfort.
After the upheaval
may heart healing begin here
in your house of prayer.

**For my house shall be called a house of
prayer for all peoples (Isa. 56:7 RSV).**

About the
—Goodness of God—

For you know the grace of our Lord
Jesus Christ, that though he was rich, yet
for your sake he became poor, so that by his
poverty you might become rich.

2 Corinthians 8:9 RSV

Glory to God

I marvel at man's inventions—
electric blanket, TV, microwave oven.
But your creative hand arouses
greater amazement.
One prize for growing old
is early wakening
that lets me hear bird song,
watch murky sky
turn geranium hued,
see tight buds poking
from violet plants.
Your world brings glory to you.

O God, nourish the tender shoots
of my love for you
so they blossom today
for your glory.

**We give thanks to thee, O God; we give
thanks: we call on thy name and recount
thy wondrous deeds (Ps. 75:1 RSV).**

Thoughts about Worship

Father in heaven,
this is your day,
and I am your child.
Prepare me for worship,
heart and mind centered on you.
Sometimes, by what they wear and whisper,
people get in the way.
Then there are announcements,
and the giving of tithes.
Help me bow my heart.
Is there anyone I need to forgive
or ask to forgive me?
Count my blessings?
Name them one by one?
With joy?
What would happen if I shouted hallelujah
in church?
Never mind. I'll sing.
Give me inner joy that spills over
in worship every day.

Not to us, O Lord, not to us but to your name be the glory, because of your love and faithfulness (Ps. 115:1 NIV).

God's Book

Thank you for protecting
the Scriptures
through the centuries.
Your Book,
written by your Holy Spirit,
tells us of your holiness,
your mighty power and love,
your judgment and mercy.
Thanks for including
biographies of men and women
who sinned and made mistakes,
repented, and were reconciled
to you.
Thanks for preserving
a record of the Savior's life
and death and resurrection.
Give me grace to listen
to your reproofs
and obey your commands.

All scripture is given by inspiration of God, and is profitable for doctrine, for reproof, for correction, for instruction in righteousness (2 Tim. 3:16 KJV).

Month's End

I'm adding up figures
and taking stock.
Something is lacking,
and it's cash.
Still, your Word teaches
true wealth is found
only in you.
All my possessions
are gifts from you.
  Yours, Lord!
  Do with them what you will.

When you remove a treasure
I value,
have you planned a better gift?
One I am too blind to see?
Lord, you give me all I need.
How wonderful are your gifts!

**Set your affection on things above, not on
things on the earth (Col. 3:2 KJV).**

Bright Prospects

What do others think of growing old
when they look at me?
  Crankiness?
  Aches and pains?
  Laziness?
I hope not.
Forbid that I should sit and wait
for a special invitation
to enjoy life.
Disturb my complacency.
Lift the littleness of my vision
to the abundant life you offer.
Let me grow old
eager for each day.
Help me forget self,
speak softly to your people,
pass on your love with joy.

Be glad in the Lord, and rejoice, O righteous, and shout for joy, all you upright in heart (Ps. 32:11 RSV).

Facing the Impossible

Some crises are too big
for me to understand.
Impossible to solve.
Thank you for the comfort
of friends.
Forgive me when I depend too much
on human help
to pull me out of slippery places.
Your resources are limitless.
Into your hands, Lord.
You be in charge.
You be the power in my life.
Oh! yes, Lord, make me willing
to accept your solution.

**With God all things are possible
(Matt. 19:26 KJV).**

Mustard Seeds and
Mulberry Trees (Luke 17:6 NIV)

How you listen and
answer prayer, Lord,
is too much for me to fathom.
Yet I know you hear when we pray
in harmony with your will
because of your Son's name.

No holding back.
  Come boldly.
  Ask, seek, knock.
No letting up.
  Pray at all times.
Little prayers:
  headaches, lost papers, weather.
Big prayers:
  Heartaches, lost friends, the future.
Prayers about mulberry trees
and mountains.
What's needed is faith, but not much.
The size of a mustard seed will do
if no obstacle stands in the way.
Faith qualified by the Savior's pledge.

**If you ask anything in my name, I will
do it (John 14:14 RSV).**

Dialog

A long life teaches
the "patience of unanswered prayer."
Often I have prayed and prayed
and waited for returns
less prompt than I would like.
But your official reply
has always arrived in time.
Again the answer comes
after a tiny feeble prayer.
You must know my need
before I do.

Dear God, I praise you
for answered prayer.
I cannot count the times
you have kept your promise
to hear me when I pray.

**Call to me and I will answer you, and will
tell you great and hidden things which you
have not known (Jer. 33:3 RSV).**

Earthquake and Sunrise

An eerie midnight tremor
awakened sleepers.
Shifting tables, chairs,
crashing lamps, pictures,
doors sprung open,
roofs pitched into rooms.
After the convulsion
people huddled, dazed and frightened,
remembering a neat and orderly life.
Morning brought
golden sun, blue sky,
and devastation.
May we be quick to give aid
while they gather up the pieces
and start living anew.

Thank you, God,
that sunrises are not occasional,
but regular.

**Your Father who is in heaven . . . makes
his sun rise on the evil and on the good,
and sends rain on the just and on the unjust
(Matt. 5:45 RSV).**

On Wings of Wind

Your world is beautiful
tonight, O God.
Thick swirls of snow
tucked in at corners
blanket dirt and dead grass.
Just so your Son's righteousness
covers me.
A shaft of heavenly poetry
slants down from lunar height.
Just so Jesus brings
light to my life.
Wind is rising,
night is closing in,
and God gives peace.

**Bless the Lord, O my soul! O Lord my
God, thou art very great! . . . who ridest on
the wings of the wind (Ps. 104:1-3 RSV).**